AI SMART KIT

AGILE DECISION-MAKING ON AI

Abridged Version

Melodena Stephens

Himanshu Vashishtha

Information Age Publishing, Inc.

"Preparing for our future is a necessity, not a luxury. Unprepared governments will suffer from missed opportunities and lost wealth" (Al Maktoum, 2016).

His Highness Sheikh Mohammed bin Rashid Al Maktoum,
Vice President and Prime Minister of the UAE,
Ruler of Dubai

AI SMART KIT

AGILE DECISION-MAKING ON AI

Abridged Version

AUTHORS

Melodena Stephens

Himanshu Vashishtha

Information Age Publishing, Inc.
www.infoagepub.com

Human Brain = 1,000 trillion connections,
86 billion neurons
Deep Learning Networks = 10–1,200 connections,
10,000 neurons (Huang et al., 2016; Richard, 2018)

Library of Congress Cataloging-in-Publication Data
A CIP record for this book is available from the Library of Congress
http://www.loc.gov

ISBN: 978-1-64802-415-3 (Paperback)
        978-1-64802-416-0 (Hardcover)
        978-1-64802-417-7 (E-Book)

Information Age Publishing, Inc.
Charlotte, NC
www.infoagepub.com

Printed in the United States of America

CONTENTS

WHAT IS AI?

The European Union (EU, 2018) refers to Artificial Intelligence (AI) as systems designed by humans that, given a complex goal, act in the physical or digital world by perceiving their environment, interpreting the collected structured or unstructured data, reasoning on the knowledge derived from this data, and deciding the best action(s) to take (according to pre-defined parameters) to achieve the given goal.

AI systems can also be designed to learn to adapt their behavior by analyzing how the environment is affected by their previous actions.

As a scientific discipline, AI includes several approaches and techniques, such as machine learning (of which deep learning and reinforcement learning are specific examples), machine reasoning (which includes planning, scheduling, knowledge representation and reasoning, search, and optimization), and robotics (which includes control, perception, sensors, and actuators, as well as the integration of all other techniques into cyber-physical systems; Andreessen Horowitz, n.d.).

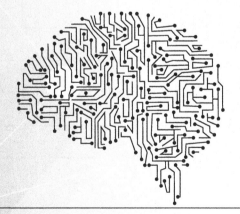

AI SMART KIT

AI MANAGER'S DILEMMA

AI promises great solutions to our earth-sized problems but with it also comes the decision maker's problem (Chen, 2017a). How would you make an effective decision about technology when you can only see surface benefits? How would you ensure the best outcome for the organization, the stakeholders, and the broader community?

These fifteen scales will help the agile manager develop decision-making skills by giving you some idea of what questions to ask in an AI project before commissioning and implementing it. It will help you think of the resources required. While all AI requires a significant amount of resource commitment to start, the scales are coded to indicate a relative degree of resource commitment (finance, time, and effort). The right hand of the scale signifies more resources. An AI project will require constant scrutiny to ensure that it is not used for the wrong reasons and all safeguards of good AI are in place.

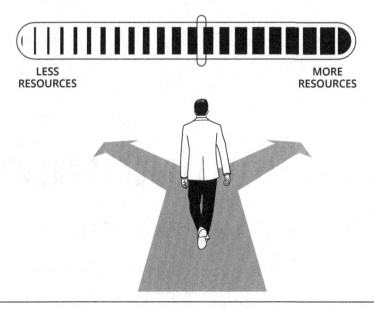

LESS
RESOURCES

MORE
RESOURCES

AI SMART KIT SCALES

"Everything we love about civilization is a product of intelligence, so amplifying our human intelligence with artificial intelligence has the potential of helping civilization flourish like never before—as long as we manage to keep the technology beneficial" (Tegmark, 2016).

Max Tegmark, president of the Future of Life Institute

LESS
RESOURCES

MORE
RESOURCES

AI SMART KIT

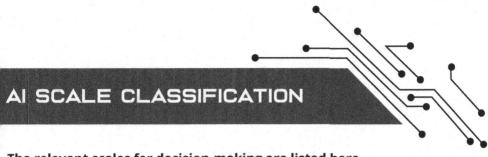

AI SCALE CLASSIFICATION

The relevant scales for decision-making are listed here.

Classification	Scale
AI Expertise	1
AI Operations	2, 3
AI Data	4, 5
AI and Employees	6, 7, 8
AI and Customers	9, 10
AI and Regulatory Environment	11, 12
AI and Responsibility	13, 14, 15

AI SMART KIT SCALES

AI EXPERTISE

SCALE 1: AI EXPERTISE LEVEL

AI expertise is the level of technology complexity the organization is using.

LESS
RESOURCES

MORE
RESOURCES

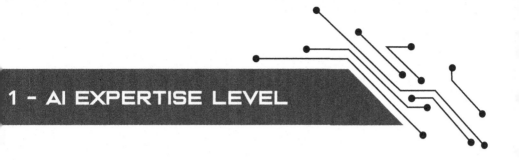

AI EXPERTISE

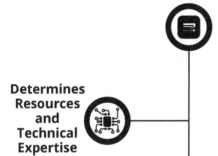

Determines Resources and Technical Expertise

NARROW OR WEAK AI	GENERAL AI OR STRONG OR BROAD AI	SUPER AI
Performs a narrow task. (Chatbots that respond to written queries or virtual assistants like Alexa or Siri)	Uses multiple domains of knowledge. (IBM Debator and autonomous cars are slowly getting to this level)	Equal to or can outperform human intelligence. Must have human consciousness. No example yet...

"Deep learning is the most fundamental advance in AI research . . . since . . . 1956 . . ."

Frank Chen (2017b), partner at Andreessen Horowitz

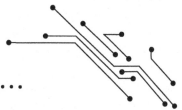

Deep learning/neural networks...
What you did not know?

"People naively believe that if you take deep learning and scale it 100 times more layers, and add 1,000 times more data, a neural net will be able to do anything a human being can do," says François Chollet, a researcher at Google, "But that's just not true" (Pontin, 2018).

Deep Learning systems are

- Greedy—demand huge sets of training data.

- Brittle—when given a "transfer test" (different scenarios from training sets), it frequently doesn't work.

- Opaque/Hidden—unlike traditional programs where you can find errors in code, here you can only look at parameters in terms of their weights within a mathematical geography.

- Shallow—as it is programmed to assume humans are rational and hence doesn't even have human common sense and can't differentiate causation from correlation (Marcus, 2017).

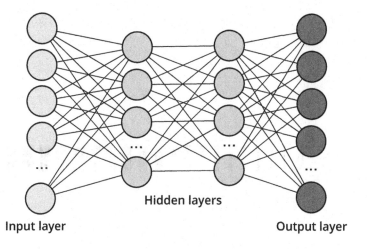

Input layer   Hidden layers   Output layer

AI OPERATIONS

SCALE 2: INTEROPERABILITY LEVEL

This is the ability of different systems to "talk" to each other.

LESS
RESOURCES

MORE
RESOURCES

INTEROPERABILITY

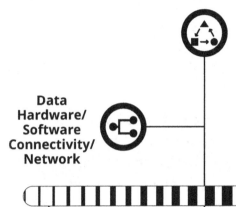

Data Hardware/ Software Connectivity/ Network

ISOLATED SYSTEMS

In a department or within an organization.

CONNECTED SYSTEMS

Using same software with suppliers and distributors.

(For example, the Alibaba platform offers its merchants advanced AI options like a virtual customer service robot, AI generated ads, financing and logistics)

UNIVERSAL SYSTEMS

Across organizations at national or international level.

(Estonia and Finland sharing medical records and prescriptions)

"Interoperability is defined as the ability of different information technology systems and software applications to communicate, exchange data, and use the information that has been exchanged."

HIMSS Insights, 2019

Why is this important?

By 2020, the 5G network will support 50 billion plus connected devices, 212 billion connected sensors, and enable access to 44 zettabytes of data allowing us to use 35% of digital data versus 5% (West, 2016).

Interoperability Considerations

Foundational/Technical Interoperability—data exchange but the interpretation is at human level. This is a technical system decision.

Structural or Syntactic Interoperability—defines common data format for exchange, whether the data is usable and can be reconciled without too much manual intervention.

Semantic or Advanced Interoperability—the layer will define the data to have a common understanding.

Pragmatic Interoperability—mutual understanding of the context and use of data across systems.

Dynamic Interoperability—the system understands changes over time.

Conceptual Interoperability—a system design decision on which everything is structured and all assumptions and constraints are known.

LEVEL	6	CONCEPTUAL INTEROPERABILITY
LEVEL	5	DYNAMIC INTEROPERABILITY
LEVEL	4	PRAGMATIC INTEROPERABILITY
LEVEL	3	SEMANTIC INTEROPERABILITY
LEVEL	2	SYNTACTIC INTEROPERABILITY
LEVEL	1	TECHNICAL INTEROPERABILITY
LEVEL	0	NO INTEROPERABILITY

INCREASING CAPACITY FOR INTEROPERATION →

AI SMART KIT SCALES

AI OPERATIONS

SCALE 3: GLOBAL EMBEDDEDNESS

This consideration requires you to evaluate systems being used "outside" your organization.

LESS
RESOURCES

MORE
RESOURCES

3 - AI AND GLOBAL EMBEDDEDNESS

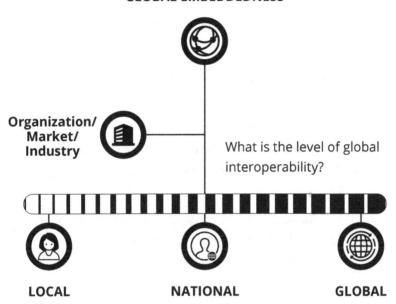

GLOBAL EMBEDDEDNESS

Organization/ Market/ Industry

What is the level of global interoperability?

LOCAL   **NATIONAL**   **GLOBAL**

For example, at an industry level you could have compatibility issues like that of Android and iOS systems, or between new product versions. COVID-19 showed a breakdown in global systems in real-time health surveillance, data for decision-making, and the limitations of extrapolating data from one context to another. International passenger travel and health data across countries became critical during the COVID-19 pandemic but it was not available.

"The most encouraging uses of AI will be in early warning of terror activities, incipient diseases and environmental threats, and in improvements in decision-making" (Pew Research, 2018).

Theodore Gordon, futurist, management consultant, and co-founder of The Millennium Project

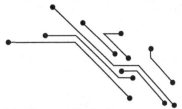

AI global race

Interesting facts based on simulations from the McKinsey Global Institute (Bughin et al., 2018)

- By 2030, AI will add US$ 13 trillion to the global GDP.

- Leading AI countries could capture an additional 20–25% in net economic benefits, while developing countries might capture only about 5–15%.

- AI will follow the S-curve of innovation—meaning its growth might be three or more times higher by 2030 than it is over the next 5 years.

- Greatest cumulative boost will come from product and service innovations and extensions (24%).

- Front-runners who have a strong digital base could have an additional annual net cash flow growth of about 6% while laggards that do not adopt AI technologies at all or that have not fully absorbed them in their enterprises by 2030, may experience a 20% decline in cash flow.

- 3% of the total wage bill could shift to categories requiring nonrepetitive and high digital skills.

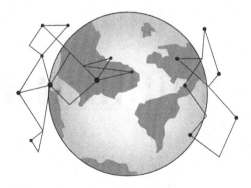

AI DATA

SCALE 4: DATA TYPES

This requires you to evaluate the data that is available for your AI.

LESS
RESOURCES

MORE
RESOURCES

DATA TYPES

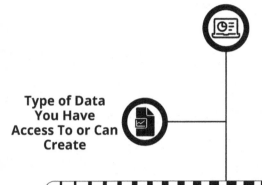

Type of Data You Have Access To or Can Create

STRUCTURED DATA

Requires some manual handling of data at compilation, verification or dispatch. Need to train the system.

STRUCTURED DYNAMIC DATA

Seamless, automated data. Is able to work with some unstructured data.

UNSTRUCTURED DATA

Seamless, harmonized, automated. Assumption: System is already well-trained and vetted quality of outputs. Requires large support of specialist teams.

We produce 2.5 quintillion bytes of data each day, 90% in the last two years alone.

(Tech Startups, 2018)

1 quintillion = 10^{18}

Ways to train data (depends on data type, time, and resources)

There are four major ways to train deep learning networks: supervised, unsupervised, semi-supervised, and reinforcement learning.

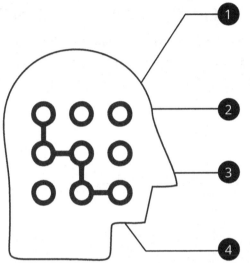

1 Supervised Learning
– here the data is structured, coded (labeled), and we already know the right answer.

2 Unsupervised Learning
– the data has no labels and you try and find patterns.

3 Semi-supervised Learning
– small amounts of labeled data and lots of unlabeled data.

4 Reinforcement Learning
– labeled data sets are not available, but you can make out if the goal is being achieved and hence use rewards or punishments to train the data.

It is a good practice to monitor your model and retrain it, based on changes in data or conditions in which that data was relevant.

AI DATA

SCALE 5: DATA MANAGEMENT

The ability for managing data (impacts hiring and outsourcing decisions) depends on the output you want.

LESS
RESOURCES

MORE
RESOURCES

DATA MANAGEMENT

Data Processing and Type of Answers It Can Give

Data Management is subject to data sets, training, and retraining

DESCRIPTIVE ANALYTICS	DIAGNOSTIC ANALYTICS	PREDICTIVE ANALYTICS	PRESCRIPTIVE ANALYTICS
What happened in the past?	Why did it happen?	What will happen?	How can it be made to happen?
Will help highlight an anomaly (for example, revenues are down by 5%), but it will not tell you why. (Tableau Software)	Used in real time data analysis. The objective is to find a relationship and tell a "story." You need to train the algorithm. (Gartner Insights)	Here you use past data to forecast the future. You need to build and validate the AI model. (traffic prediction, peak capacities and Netflix user preferences)	Based on past data, the output information is used to influence choice selection. The model has a feedback loop for constant (re)learning. (self-driving cars; airlines and hotels dynamic pricing)

"Data is Messy"

Andrew Ng, CEO of Landing, founder of
www.deeplearning.ai (Ng, 2019)

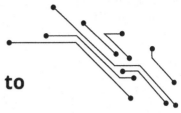

When managing data, you need to look at these questions:

1. What is the level of simplification and at what cost? Can you make decision choices easy? Is the system allowing free decisions or is it forcing choices?

2. Are there any blind spots? What was left out? Was it important? How do you know?

3. Have you considered the long tail of probability? This is to ensure you are not biasing the system, and understand how outliers work. You do not want to discriminate.

4. What is the level of transparency that you want? What are the decision criteria? Can there be errors?

5. What is your legal responsibility to data you do not own but can access?

6. What is your legal and moral responsibility to data you collect?

Data analytics is dependent on the quality of the data (Jeff Bezos as cited in Bort, 2019) and hence there is an inherent bias. Only 3% of data in an organization meets the quality for analytics (Nagle et al., 2017). Important to note here that correlation does not mean causation.

AI & EMPLOYEES

SCALE 6: AI AND HUMAN TEAMS

This decides the level of coordination and integration of AI in the workplace.

LESS
RESOURCES

MORE
RESOURCES

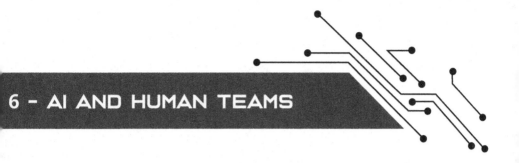

AI-HUMAN TEAMS

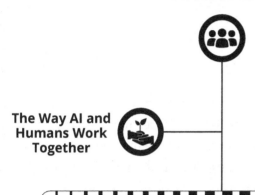

The Way AI and Humans Work Together

AI WORKS UNDER SUPERVISION OF HUMAN	AI AND HUMAN WORK AS A TEAM	AI WORKS INDEPENDENT OF HUMAN	AI IS TAKING DECISIONS INDEPENDENT OF HUMAN
Human controls the AI.	Almost in equal partnership, often with different roles.	Alerting human in terms of breakdown.	Human gets consolidated report.

"Overall we should be focusing much more energy on the quality of jobs and the meaning of human activity in general, and we must be vigilant when it may come to the reduction of human autonomy due to the deployment of AI."

Marek Havrda, AI Policy & Social Impact Director, GoodAI (World Government Summit 2019)

Garry Kasporov was the world chess champion. Between 1985–1996, he defeated all chess computers including Deep Blue, a US$ 10 million IBM computer. This was then reprogrammed and defeated him in 1997.

When IBM declined a rematch, Garry went on to create Centaur Chess, which was a competition of teams of AI and humans. He soon concluded that "weak human + machine + better process was superior to a strong computer alone and, more remarkable, superior to a strong human + machine + inferior process" (Cowen, 2014; Kasparov, 2008; Rasskin-Gutman and Klosky, 2009). Perhaps the reason is complimentability—as general intelligence is said to account only for 30–50% of any cognitive task (Deary, 2000).

This teaming up of man and machine in the age of AI requires a flexible social interaction, trust, and a robust understanding of the rules of a free society (Wagner, 2020). A computer excels in rationalizing a process. At this point, AI does not have a moral compass, and AI cannot be punished the same way humans can for breaking laws, so we need to proceed with caution. Currently, significant research is being undertaken to teach AI social intelligence (DARPA, 2019).

AI & EMPLOYEES

SCALE 7: HUMAN PRODUCTIVITY

This is to help understand how AI will contribute to the human workforce.

LESS
RESOURCES

MORE
RESOURCES

HUMAN PRODUCTIVITY

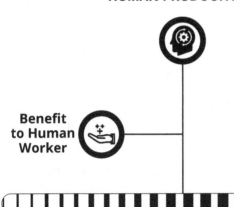

Benefit to Human Worker

ENHANCING EFFICIENCY

Performs a narrow task, works on efficiency, suitable for repetitive tasks, or where there is not enough talent. It frees humans for more decision-making and customized solutions.

(car factories—robots for painting, welding, or assembly)

ENHANCING/ ASSISTING DECISION-MAKING

Is able to help humans in decision-making; in some cases, takes decisions based on a set of clearly specified rules.

(at an individual level—autonomous driving; at a wider level—traffic systems or smart cities)

SUBSTITUTION (INTUITIVE)

Equal to or can outperform human intelligence. Could lead to job replacement and unemployment. Needs tremendous caution.

"People will increasingly realize the importance of interacting with each other and the natural world and they will program AI to support such goals, which will in turn support the ongoing emergence of the 'slow movement'" (Pew Research, 2018).

Dana Klisanin, psychologist, futurist, and game designer

AI is "about reimagining processes in ways that weren't possible before." James Wilson, Accenture (Wilson & Daugherty, 2018)

A business survey on AI (as quoted in the ICT Enterprise Survey on Artificial Intelligence, 2018), found that:

 **92**%

 **77**%

 **66**%

 **28**%

| hoped AI would bring improved efficiency across the board. | expected to see a reduction in overall costs. | anticipated enhanced accuracy in their operations. | believed that AI will enable humans to make the most of their creative side. |

AI & EMPLOYEES

SCALE 8: ONBOARDING

This is to determine the scope and costs of onboarding AI.

LESS
RESOURCES

MORE
RESOURCES

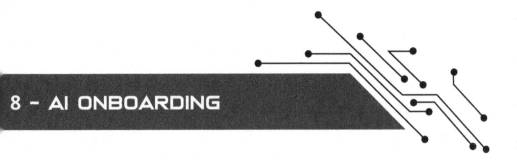

AI ONBOARDING

Onboarding Considerations

- Time to Learn
- Time to implement New Systems, Structures
- Developing New Roles
- Deploying New Governance Structures

How Do You Get AI Accepted?
Human-centered approach

WITHIN THE ORGANIZATION

Organization and customers can switch with minimum training. Easy to integrate across departments.

AT INDUSTRY AND NATIONAL LEVEL

AI is easy to integrate with the existing systems in the organization and outside with industry and at the national level.

ACROSS INDUSTRIES AND COUNTRIES

AI is easy to use and to co-create leading to more collaboration.

Training, user designed systems, and a culture that understands data and its limitations.

"The thing I have noticed is when the anecdotes and the data disagree, the anecdotes are usually right. There's something wrong with the way you are measuring it" (Bezos, 2018).

Jeff Bezos, founder and CEO of Amazon

AI SMART KIT

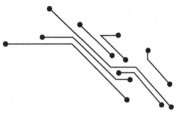

What you need for successful AI onboarding

- **AI training:**
  You should make sure that all employees taking decisions on AI, using AI, or being affected by AI, are trained on issues highlighted before: Have general information sessions, understand the data you have, and the ways AI can contribute to the organization or impact the broader society.

- **AI buy-in:**
  Do a deep dive into business and technical feasibility of AI projects and get ownership across teams.

- **Pilot projects:**
  Test, test, test and learn, relearn, and retrain AI.

- **Develop an AI strategy:**
  What you want to achieve and how you want to achieve it.

- **Develop internal competencies:**
  As you scale, you will need to have in-house AI talent.

- **Legal and Governance:**
  Build as you scale up and across countries.

- **Outreach:**
  Take a leadership role in AI and reach out to other institutions (at the industry, national, and global level).

AI & CUSTOMERS

SCALE 9: SENSORY EXPERIENCE

This helps determine the extent of immersive experience AI is providing.

LESS
RESOURCES

MORE
RESOURCES

SENSORY EXPERIENCE

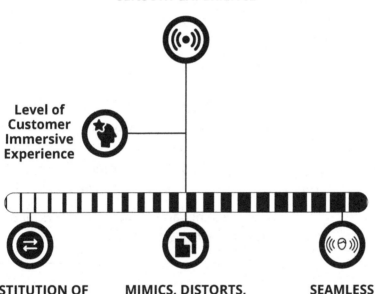

Level of Customer Immersive Experience

SUBSTITUTION OF FEW SENSES

Substitutes your senses partially.

(haptic technology—your keypad on your smart phone)

MIMICS, DISTORTS, OR AUGMENTS

Multi-sense (immersion)— vision, auditory, tactile, olfaction, gustation . . .

(use of immersive technology or implanted technology)

SEAMLESS

Cannot make a distinction between reality and virtual/AI experience. (Estonia's virtual government & proactive invisible services using AI for life events)

"AI is creating a world where reality can be manipulated in ways we do not appreciate. Fake videos, audio, and similar media, are likely to explode and create a world where 'reality' is hard to discern" (Pew Research, 2018).

Thad Hall, a researcher and coauthor of *Politics for a Connected American Public*

- **Areas of application**
  - Education (training and teaching), medicine (diagnostics, scenario planning, rehabilitation, etc.), tourism (virtual tourism), communication (meetings, information, and idea transfer), entertainment (think Pokémon Go), retail, digital eyewear, security training, automobiles (for example see Kelly, 2016).

- **Data and sensory overload**
  - There may be 463 exabytes of data generated daily by 2025. At the beginning of 2020 total digital data till date is 44,000 exabytes.

- **Ethics Question**
  - Do virtual and immersive worlds distort our perception of reality and how important is it for us to separate the two?

AI & CUSTOMERS

SCALE 10: HUMAN INTERFACE

Determines what level of AI integration with the human beings is desired.

LESS
RESOURCES

MORE
RESOURCES

10 - AI AND THE HUMAN INTERFACE

HUMAN INTERFACE

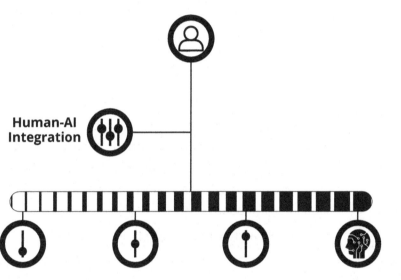

Human-AI Integration

LOW

AI and human are separate and interface is optional.

(Wearables)

MEDIUM

AI and human are separate but interface is necessary for access to important services needed to live a normal life.

(ATMs or mobiles)

HIGH

AI and human are not separate and interface adds to the perceived quality of life.

(Pacemaker)

TRANS-SPECIES?

AI and human are not separate and interface considered part of human.

(Cyborgs of the future? Neil Harbinsson)

"If the goal of future education is to facilitate the development of 'wise cyborgs,' then the 'solutions to modern global challenges require a synthesis of holistic, integrative, future-focused, and ethical thinking—all qualities of wisdom.'"

(Lombard and Blackwood, 2011)

AI SMART KIT

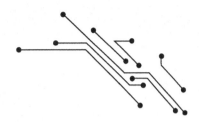

The AI–human interface can help augment your current human capabilities like speaking, writing, hearing, seeing, perceiving, and can provide real-time diagnostics (analysis and prediction).

Neil Harbinsson had an antenna implanted in his skull in 2004 as a sensory device to help him perceive color but it can send information to him even from satellites. He calls himself a cyborg and hence is trans-species.

These new technologies will change the way we lie but they also leave many questions for regulators and societies as we wish them to be (Blake & Polidoro, 2016).

AI & REGULATORY ENVIRONMENT

SCALE 11: REGULATIONS

AI regulations need to have a human centric approach.

LESS
RESOURCES

MORE
RESOURCES

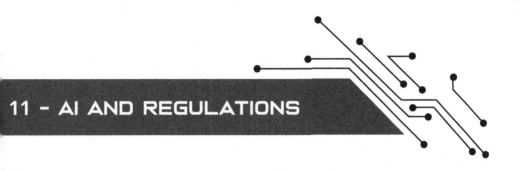

AI REGULATIONS

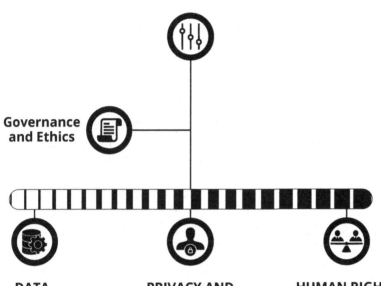

Governance and Ethics

DATA

Security, integrity, and bias.

PRIVACY AND PERMISSION

Compliance with rules and ethical norms.

HUMAN RIGHTS

Ensuring data collection and use cannot violate fundamental human rights.

AI regulations will be a critical component of successful implementation. These could be at organizational, industry, or national levels.

"By far, the greatest danger of Artificial Intelligence is that people conclude too early that they understand it" (Yudkowsky, 2008)

Eliezer Yudkowsky, Research Fellow, Machine Intelligence Research Institute

Many governments, like the EU are trying to understand and work on AI regulations and ethics (Commission on Civil Law Rules on Robotics, 2017). For example, the EU General Data Protection Regulation and the Chinese Social Credit System may look at two ends of privacy. Who could have foreseen that social media websites (free to the consumer) were able to "sell" customer data and this would lead to fake news? While much of the data is in the hands of private companies, the fight on 5G and which country owns the tech and which country do you trust most with citizen data will be an interesting debate for future trade wars. This issue of trust is applicable to companies. In many cases, customers feel that they have no choice in accepting the conditions laid out for use of the service. This will eventually lead to regulations that affect companies with access to data and those that use data for AI. As we have seen in recent times, perception is everything.

AI & REGULATORY ENVIRONMENT

SCALE 12: INTELLECTUAL PROPERTY (IP)

Determining the level of IP protection the organization wants.

LESS
RESOURCES

MORE
RESOURCES

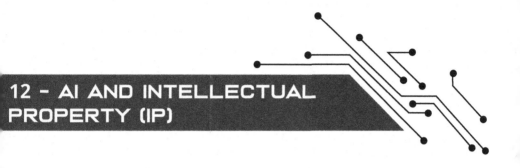

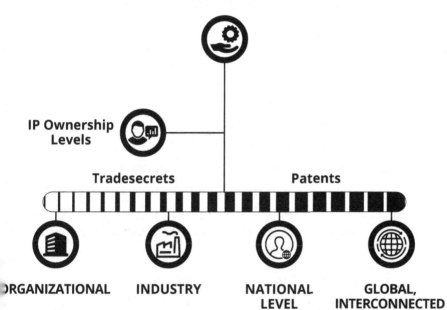

IP/OWNERSHIP

IP Ownership Levels

Tradesecrets

Patents

ORGANIZATIONAL   INDUSTRY   NATIONAL LEVEL   GLOBAL, INTERCONNECTED LEVEL

Competitive advantage can come from hardware, software, algorithms, trademarks, data, data relationships, etc.
Roles organizations can take are owner, broker, governance keeper, gatekeeper, and custodian.

The European Parliament resolution of February 16, 2017 with recommendations to the Commission on Civil Law Rules on Robotics not only talks about the need to define a "robot" but the principles concerning the development of robotics and AI. With respect to IP, Article 18 highlights "there are no legal provisions that specifically apply to robotics, but that existing legal regimes and doctrines can be readily applied to robotics."

Who owns the IP that AI creates?

Who owns the data? Who owns the tech?

Who owns personal digital data—the person who creates it, who it is about, or those who collect it?

AI now can create output but it cannot be copyrighted as, currently, the law says it must have a human author (Scalla, 2018).

Since 1965, there are 1.6 million AI-related scientific publications and filed patent applications for nearly 340,000 AI-related inventions (40% are on machine learning; WIPO, n.d.). Of the top 500 AI patent applications, companies owned 333 (33% based in the U.S.), universities and public research organizations owned 167 (66% in China; WIPO, n.d.).

AI Applications Fields (WIPO, n.d.)

#1
Telecommunications
51,273 applications
(15%)

#2
Transport
50,861 applications
(15%)

#3
Life and Medical Sciences
40,758 applications
(12%)

AI & RESPONSIBILITY

SCALE 13: IMPACT ON SUSTAINABLE DEVELOPMENT

Decides the desired balance between the cost of AI and its benefits, with AI's positive and negative impact on SDGs.

LESS
RESOURCES

MORE
RESOURCES

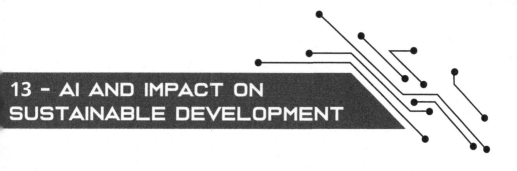

13 - AI AND IMPACT ON SUSTAINABLE DEVELOPMENT

IMPACT (SDGs)

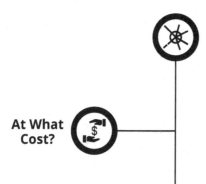

At What
Cost?

WITHIN THE
ORGANIZATION

WITHIN THE
INDUSTRY

AT THE
NATIONAL
LEVEL

AT THE GLOBAL,
INERCONNECTED
LEVEL

"AI is not a silver bullet for all of humanity's problems. But it has the potential to be a formidable tool in the toolkit. For that to happen, we need to encourage the development of applications, and push for them to be used at scale in a responsible and thoughtful manner."

(McKinsey Global Institute, 2019)

There are 17 Sustainable Development Goals (SDGs) we are committed to in the interest of global citizenship. On one hand, productivity may come at the cost of work. SDG Goal 8 states: *Promote sustained, inclusive and sustainable economic growth, full and productive employment and decent work for all.* What is decent work in the world of AI? Take another often cited goal—saving the environment (Goal 12, Goal 15). Going paperless does not help if you do not reduce your emails. A normal email has a footprint of 4g of CO_2 (due to the power data centers and the energy computers spend sending, filtering, and reading messages) while an email with a large attachment can have a carbon footprint of 50g CO_2 (Berners-Lee, 2010). One single sheet of paper produces roughly 5g of CO_2 (Fuji Xerox, n.d.).

AI & RESPONSIBILITY

SCALE 14: ACCOUNTABILITY

This decides at what level the accountability for AI is managed.

LESS
RESOURCES

MORE
RESOURCES

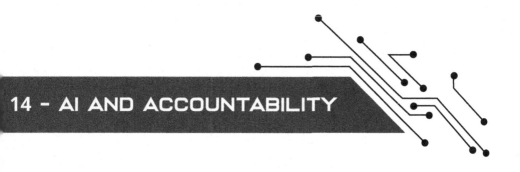

AI ACCOUNTABILITY

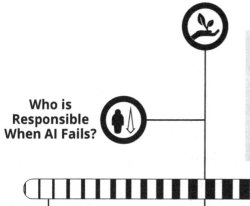

Who is Responsible When AI Fails?

If the AI fails or has a negative effect on consumers, employees, or society—who will take responsibility for implementing that decision?

WITHIN THE TECHNICAL DEPARTMENT AND THE DEPARTMENT THAT SOURCES THE AI

WITHIN THE DEPARTMENT THAT USES THE SERVICE

AI SENIOR MANAGEMENT

Keep in mind, no matter what we think AI is—it is still not capable of functioning as a human, which leads to AI bad behaviors. If you think of AI as a teenager, then as a parent (decision maker), you are still accountable. Someone is.

"The greatest benefit of the arrival of artificial intelligence is that AIs will help define humanity. We need AIs to tell us who we are" (Kelly, 2016).

Kevin Kelly, cofounder of *Wired*

AI Responsibility

A considerable amount of work is being done in this area. Some areas of consideration are:

1. Data privacy
2. Data biases
3. AI security (for AI itself and the humans involved in any part of the process)
4. AI transparency and explainability (How is it ensured that mistakes are caught and can be rectified as quickly as possible in the decision taking process?)
5. AI control and accountability (Who is responsible, can the human intervene and stop AI, at what stages, what are risks and risk management procedures and what happens to data and decisions at the end of the AI lifecycle?)
6. AI and human rights (Though this is well outlined—even the right to take decisions, autonomy, and human dignity must be considered.)
7. AI and conformity to "do no harm"

AI & RESPONSIBILITY

SCALE 15: CRISES
PREPAREDNESS

This decides how prepared we are for AI crises.

LESS
RESOURCES

MORE
RESOURCES

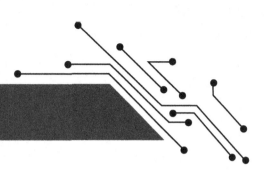

CRISES PREPAREDNESS

Three levels of Cybersecurity

- Readiness strategy (within the organization and with other organizations)
- Defence strategy (If attacked what will you do?)
- Intelligence (How will this feed into first two points?)

Planning Level

TECHNICAL

Software and hardware security and protection

DATA

Data integrity and security, compliance and governance

KNOWLEDGE

Expertise, history and minimum functioning capabilities

For crises preparedness, look for compatibility issues, obsolescence, and cybersecurity. The government of Estonia (e-Estonia) has a Data Embassy as a cloud extension of the government stored in another country (Luxembourg). It will allow the government to operate even if something happened to the physical country.

"The real risk of AI isn't malice but competence" (Hawking, 2015)

Stephen Hawking

Crises are inevitable...all you can do is be prepared

- for failure of power, tech, human—AI teams;
- for security breaches and cyber attacks;
- for data inadequacies and data misrepresentation;
- for legal and ethical scandals;
- for moral dilemma and those products that offend the ethos of the culture of the company, community, society, or nation;
- for breaches in due diligence; and
- for AI or digital twins, misrepresenting the human person.

SOURCES

Andreessen Horowitz. (n.d.). *AI playbook, Microsite.* Retrieved from http://aiplaybook.a16z.com

Berners-Lee, M. (2010). *How bad are bananas: The carbon footprint of everything.* Vancouver, Canada: Greystone Books.

Bezos J. (2018). *Forum on Leadership: A Conversation with Jeff Bezos* [video]. Retrieved from, https://www.youtube.com/watch?v=xu6vFIKAUxk&feature=youtu.be

Blake, P., & Polidoro, R. (2016, September 14). Exclusive: Why Apple CEO Tim Cook prefers augmented reality over virtual reality. *Good Morning America.* Retrieved from https://abcnews.go.com/Technology/exclusive-apple-ceo-tim-cook-prefers-augmented-reality/story?id=42064913

Bort, J. (2018, April 21). Amazon CEO Jeff Bezos explains his famous one-character emails, known to strike fear in managers' hearts, *Business Insider.* Retrieved from https://www.businessinsider.com/bezos-explains-his-dreaded-one-character-emails-2018-4

Bughin, J., Seong, J., Manyika, J., Chui, M., & Joshi, R. (2018, September 4). "Notes from the AI frontier: Modeling the impact of AI on the world economy." *McKinsey Global Institute.* Retrieved from https://www.mckinsey.com/featured-insights/artificial-intelligence/notes-from-the-ai-frontier-modeling-the-impact-of-ai-on-the-world-economy

Chen, F. (2017a). *AI: What's working, what's not?* [video]. Retrieved from

https://a16z.com/2017/12/07/summit-ai-update-frank-chen/

Chen, F. (2017b, July 15). *The promise of AI (2017); AI, deep learning, and machine learning: A primer* [Youtube]. Retrieved from https://www.youtube.com/watch?v=8pLZkbN9h_s

Commission on Civil Law Rules on Robotics. (2017). European Parliament. Retrieved from http://www.europarl.europa.eu/doceo/document/TA-8-2017-0051_EN.html?redirect

Cowen, T. (2014). *Average is over: Powering America beyond the age of the great stagnation.* New York, NY: Penguin Putnam Inc.

DARPA. (2019). *Using AI to build better human-machine teams.* Retrieved from https://www.darpa.mil/news-events/2019-03-21b

Deary I.J. (2000). *Looking down on human intelligence: From psychometrics to the brain.* Oxford, England: Oxford University Press. doi:10.1093/acprof:oso/9780198524175.001.0001

European Commission. (2018). *Draft ethics guidelines for trustworthy AI. The European Commission's high-level expert group on artificial intelligence* [working paper]. Brussels.

European Parliament resolution of 16 February 2017 with recommendations to the Commission on Civil Law Rules on Robotics (2015/2103(INL) =, https://eur-lex.europa.eu/legal-content/EN/TXT/?uri=CELEX%3A52017IP0051

AI SMART KIT

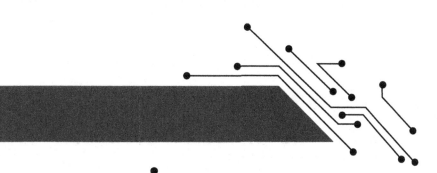

Fuji Xerox. (n.d.). *Case 1: Comparison of CO2 emissions from an environmental perspective.* Retrieved from https://www.fujixerox.com/eng/company/technology/production/ma/electronic_media/case1.html

Havrda, M. (2019). AI Policy & Social Impact Director, GoodAI, World Government Summit. https://www.goodai.com/takeaways-from-the-world-government-summit-2019/

Hawking, S. (2015). https://www.reddit.com/r/science/comments/3nyn5i/science_ama_series_stephen_hawking_ama_answers/

HIMSS Insights. (2019). *What is interoperability.* Retrieved from https://www.himss.org/resources/interoperability-healthcare

Huang G., Sun, Y., Liu, Z., Sedra, D., & Weinberger, K. (2016, March 30). *Deep networks with stochastic depth.* Retrieved from https://arxiv.org/abs/1603.09382v1

ICT Enterprise Survey on Artificial Intelligence (2018), https://aibusiness.com/document.asp?doc_id=760495

Kasparov, G. (2008). *How life imitates chess: Making the right moves, from the board to the boardroom.* With assistance of Mig Greengard. London, England: Arrow Books.

Kelly, K. (2016). *The Inevitable: Understanding the 12 technological forces that will shape our future.* New York, NY: Penguin Books.

Lombard, T., & Blackwood, R. T. (2011). Educating the wise cyborg of the future. *On the Horizon, 19*(2), 85–96.

Mack, E. (n.d.). *These 27 expert predictions about artificial intelligence will both disturb and excite you, Inc.* Retrieved from https://www.inc.com/eric-mack/heres-27-expert-predictions-on-how-youll-live-with-artificial-intelligence-in-near-future.html

Marcus, G. (2017). *Deep learning: A critical appraisal.* Retrieved from https://arxiv.org/pdf/1801.00631.pdf

McKinsey Global Institute. (2019, January 21). *Using AI to help achieve Sustainable Development Goals.* UNDP. Retrieved from https://www.undp.org/content/undp/en/home/blog/2019/Using_AI_to_help_achieve_Sustainable_Development_Goals.html

Mohammed, His Highness Sheikh Mohammed. (2016). https://twitter.com/hhshkmohd/status/797808145162715136?lang=en, Twitter, @HHShkMohd, Nov 13, 2016

Nagle, T., Redman, T. C., & Sammon, D. (2017, September 11). Only 3% of companies' data meets basic quality standards, *Harvard Business Review.* Retrieved from https://hbr.org/2017/09/only-3-of-companies-data-meets-basic-quality-standards

Ng, A. (2019). AI for Everyone. *Coursera.* Available https://www.coursera.org/learn/ai-for-everyone

Pew Research (2018). *Improvements ahead: How humans and AI might evolve together in the next decade.* Quotes complied by Anderson, J and Raine, L. Available: https://www.pewresearch.org/internet/2018/12/10/improvements-ahead-how-humans-and-ai-might-evolve-together-in-the-next-decade/

SOURCES

Pontin, J. (2018, February 2). *Greedy, brittle, opaque, and shallow: The downsides to deep learning.* Retrieved from https://www.wired.com/story/greedy-brittle-opaque-and-shallow-the-downsides-to-deep-learning/

Rasskin-Gutman, D., & Klosky, D. (2009). *Chess metaphors: Artificial intelligence and the human mind.* Boston, MA: MIT Press.

Richard, N. (2018, September 4). *The differences between artificial and biological neural networks.* Retrieved from https://towardsdatascience.com/the-differences-between-artificial-and-biological-neural-networks-a8b46db828b7

Scalla, T. (2018, September 4). *Data Ownership* (CIGI Paper No. 187). Retrieved from https://www.cigionline.org/publications/data-ownership

Tech Startups. (2018, May 21). *How much data do we create every day?* [Infographic]. Retrieved from https://techstartups.com/2018/05/21/how-much-data-do-we-create-every-day-infographic/

Tegmark, M. (2016). https://futureoflife.org/background/benefits-risks-of-artificial-intelligence/?cn-reloaded=1, Website. Futureoflife.org.

Wagner, D.N (2020). Strategically managing the artificially intelligent firm. *Strategy & Leadership, 48*(3) 19–25.

West, D. M. (2016, July 14). *How 5G technology enables the health internet of things.* Center for Technology Innovation at Brookings. Retrieved from https://www.brookings.edu/research/how-5g-technology-enables-the-health-internet-of-things/

Wilson, H. J., & Daugherty, P. R. (2018). *Human + machine: Reimagining work in the age of AI.* https://search.ebscohost.com/login.aspx?direct=true&scope=site&db=nlebk&db=nlabk&AN=1798833.

WIPO. (n.d.). *The story of AI in patents.* Retrieved from https://www.wipo.int/tech_trends/en/artificial_intelligence/story.html

Yudhkowsky, E. (2008). *Artificial intelligence as a positive and negative factor in global risk.* Machine Intelligence Research Institute. Retrieved from http://yudkowsky.net/singularity/ai-risk/a

AI SMART KIT

Printed in the United States
by Baker & Taylor Publisher Services